This book belongs to

_____

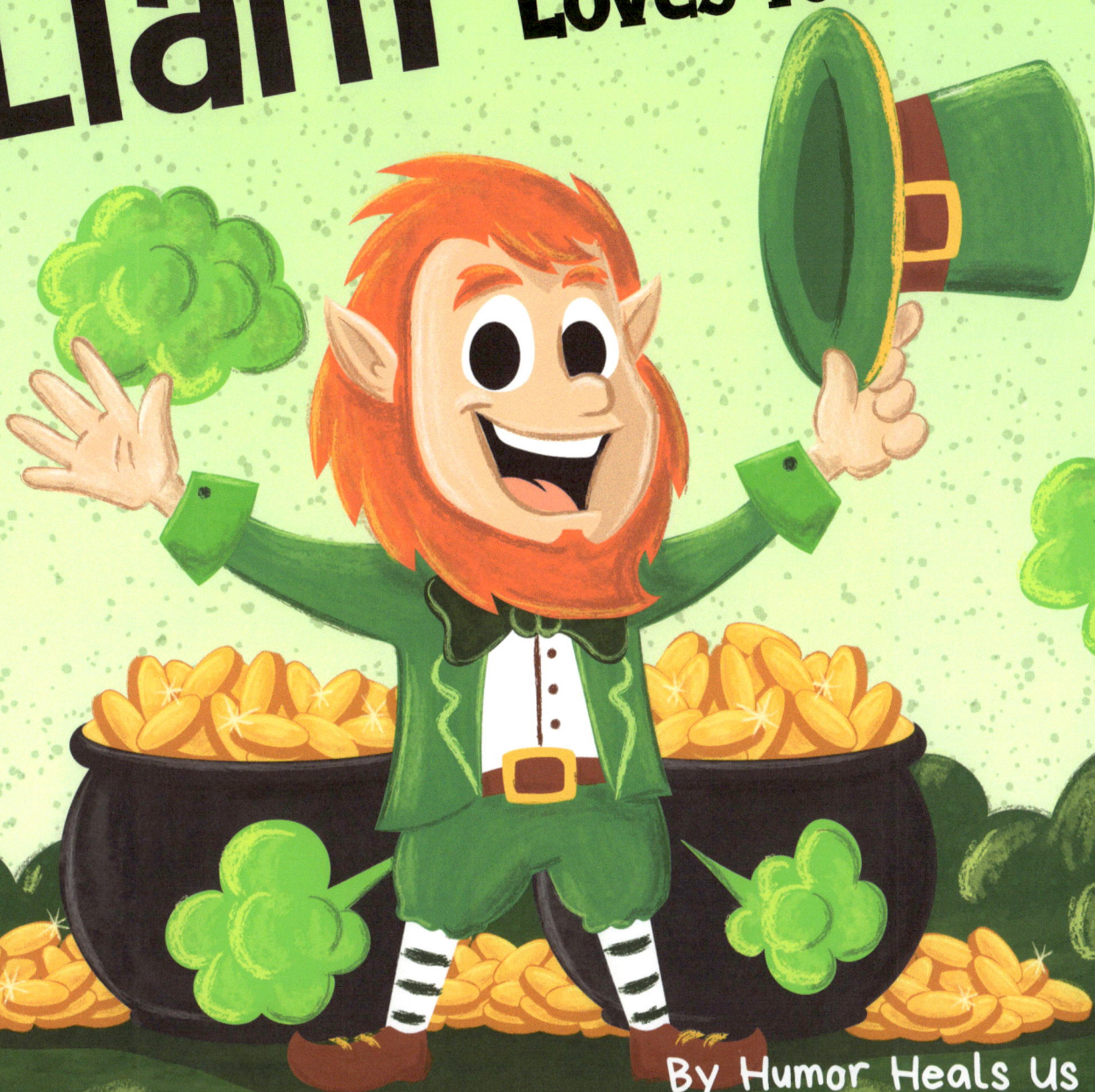

Leprechauns are like small elves.
They always dress in green.
They're mischievous and magical,
And rarely ever seen.

They have a hidden pot of gold
At the end of the rainbow.
But if you try to follow them,
You won't have any luck, no!

Liam is a leprechaun
With a very special skill.
He does amazing **magic** farts.
The smell could almost kill.

His farts are loud and powerful,
And also very smelly.
So be careful not to get too close,
Or your knees will turn to jelly.

If people try to force him
To lead them to his gold,
A **magic** fart he'll soon let rip.
Then, they won't be so bold.

They'll grab their nose and hold their breath,
And quickly run away.
All attempts to find his gold
Will need to wait for another day.

His farts can shoot him up in the air.
And with one mighty **blow**,
Liam will **fly** across the sky
Holding on to a beautiful rainbow.

Leprechauns are sneaky.
They visit homes at night.
In their constant search for gold,
If you wake they'll flee in **fright**.

But Liam Leprechaun does not sneak well.
Although he tries his best
People wake up when he farts,
So finding gold's a test.

One day some evil ogres
Found Liam's pot of gold.
They planned to steal it and be rich,
But that plan did not unfold.

For Liam Leprechaun was prepared.
He faced them with his rear,
And let off stinky magic farts
That made the ogres flee in tears.

Now Liam guards all pots of gold
Because of his **brave** acts.
With his powerful secret weapon,
He fends off all attacks.

Liam now gets a percentage
Of all the gold they find
Because he's the **keeper** of the pots
And has to stay behind.

He found a lucky four-leaf clover
And jumped around in glee.
But a sudden fart blew one leaf off,
And now there's only **Three**.

Leprechauns like all things green
In their food and drink.
But no matter what poor Liam eats,
His magic farts still **stink**.

Leprechauns are pranksters.
They're always playing tricks.
Liam sneaks up unannounced,
And farts loudly for kicks.

Even in the swimming pool,
When there's no sign of trouble,
Liam does a silent fart
And makes a big wave bubble.

One day they held a meeting,
All the leaders of the Leprechaun Nation.
Liam released such a huge fart,
It caused **mass** evacuation.

Now Liam wears a letter "F"
On his pants wherever he goes.
It's a warning he's a FARTER,
So everybody knows.

So, if you see a leprechaun
With an "F" upon his pants,
It doesn't mean his name is Fred,
And don't let him near your plants.

'Cause if he farts, your plants will wilt,
And they'll probably die.
Or else he'll take off like a flash
Across the rainbow sky.

Liam the Farting Leprechaun
Is sure a sight to see.
But he's much better **seen** then smelled,
And that's a tip from me!

Follow us on FB and IG @humorhealsus
To vote on new title names and freebies, visit
us at humorhealsus.com for more information.

@humorhealsus   @humorhealsus

www.ingramcontent.com/pod-product-compliance
Lightning Source LLC
Chambersburg PA
CBHW042025090426
42811CB00016B/1749